Peter Lacey
West Hoboken
N.J.

A MEDIÆVAL MYSTIC

NIHIL OBSTAT

F. OSMUND COONEY, O.F.M.

*Provincial
Censor Deputatus.*

IMPRIMATUR

EDMUNDUS CANONICUS SURMONT

Vicarius Generalis.

WESTMONASTERII

DIE 17 OCTOBRIS 1910

Jan van Ruysbroeck

A MEDIÆVAL MYSTIC

A SHORT ACCOUNT OF THE LIFE
AND WRITINGS OF BLESSED JOHN
RUYSBROECK, CANON REGULAR OF
GROENENDAEL A.D. 1293–1381

BY

DOM VINCENT J. SCULLY, C.R.L.

(*Permissu Superiorum*)

NEW YORK
BENZIGER BROTHERS
1911

PRINTED BY HAZELL, WATSON AND VINEY, LD., LONDON AND AYLESBURY,
FOR THOMAS BAKER, 72, NEWMAN STREET, LONDON, W.

TO

THE RIGHT REV. AUGUSTIN H. WHITE, C.R.L.

LORD ABBOT OF WALTHAM

CONTENTS

	PAGE
INTRODUCTION	ix
I. EARLY YEARS AND EDUCATION	1
II. AS A SECULAR PRIEST IN BRUSSELS	6
III. FALSE MYSTICS	10
IV. THE HERMITAGE OF GROENENDAEL	17
V. THE CANONS REGULAR OF GROENENDAEL	25
VI. PRIOR OF GROENENDAEL	33
VII. RUYSBROECK'S TREE	43
VIII. A DIRECTOR OF SOULS	47
IX. RUYSBROECK AND GERARD GROOTE	50
X. RUYSBROECK AND WINDESHEIM	58
XI. THE WRITINGS OF RUYSBROECK	67

		PAGE
XII.	THE TEACHING OF RUYSBROECK	93
XIII.	SOME APPRECIATIONS	105
XIV.	LAST DAYS	118
XV.	THE CULTUS OF BLESSED JOHN RUYSBROECK	124

INTRODUCTION

THE object of the following unpretentious little volume is to give a simple and readable account in English of the life and writings of a remarkable Flemish Mystic of the fourteenth century, a contemporary of our own Walter Hilton. Though his memory and honour have never faded in his own native Belgium, and though France and Germany have vied with each other in spreading his teaching and singing his praises, the very name of Blessed John Ruysbroeck is practically unknown this side of the water. We are acquainted with only one small work in English dealing directly with the Saint or his work at all, viz. *Reflections from the Mirror* *of Mystic*,* giving the briefest sketch of his life and some short extracts from his writings as translated from the French rendering of Ernest Hello.

The original authorities for the history of Ruysbroeck are practically reduced to one, the biography by Henry Pomerius, a Canon Regular of Groenendael, entitled *De Origine monasterii Viridisvallis una cum vitis B. Joannis Rusbrochii primi prioris hujus monasterii et aliquot coaetaneorum ejus*, re-edited by the Bollandists, Brussels, 1885. It is certain that a disciple of John Ruysbroeck, John of Scoenhoven, also of Groenendael, who undertook the defence of Blessed John's writings against Gerson, composed a short biography, but this was embodied in the work of Pomerius, and thereby as a separate volume fell out of use and memory. Pomerius

* By Earle Bailie. London: Thomas Baker. 1905.

had Scoenhoven's MS. to work upon, and some of Ruysbroeck's contemporaries were still living at Groenendael when he composed his biography there. The brief references by the Venerable Thomas à Kempis in his *Vita Gerardi Magni* are likewise of great interest and intrinsic worth.

For the purposes of this brief biography, which lays no claim whatever to original research, the compiler has made very great use of the labours of Dr. Auger, *De Doctrina et Meritis Joannis van Ruysbroeck*, Louvain, and Willem de Vreese, *Jean de Ruysbroeck*, an extract from the *Biographie Nationale*, published by l'Académie royale des sciences, des lettres et des beaux-arts de Belgique, Brussels, 1909. This indebtedness is especially true of the summarised analysis of the various works of Ruysbroeck.

Later it may be possible to give a complete and faithful English rendering of all

Ruysbroeck's Works from the critical edition which is at present preparing in Louvain, where there is an active revival of interest in this great and holy Mystic of the Netherlands.

For the judgment of competent witnesses as to the permanent value and extraordinary sublimity of B. John's writings the reader is referred to the body of this work under the heading, *Some Appreciations*.

The usual protest is made according to the Decrees of Urban VIII. concerning alleged miracles, etc., recorded in these pages.

St. Ives, Cornwall,
Feast of Our Lady's Nativity, 1910.

A Mediæval Mystic

I

EARLY YEARS AND EDUCATION

BLESSED John Ruysbroeck, surnamed the Admirable and the Divine Doctor, by common consent the greatest Mystic the Low Countries have ever produced, was born, A.D. 1293, at Ruysbroeck, a village some miles south of Brussels, lying between that city and Hal. According to the fashion of those days, especially with Religious, he was named after his birthplace, John van Ruysbroeck, or John Ruysbroeck. The Venerable à Kempis, the Latinised form of van Kempen, is a case in point ; Thomas was so named after his native town, Kempen, though his patronymic was Haemerken. Of Ruysbroeck, however, we know of no other surname; neither do his biographers so much as mention his father. But like many another great servant of God, John was blessed with a good mother, a devout woman who trained her child from the cradle to walk in the paths of Christian piety and perfection. She is charged with only one fault, that she loved her son too tenderly!

Perhaps we are to understand by this that the poor woman opposed the boy's early aspirations after a more retired life than could be found even in the peaceful shelter of his own pious home. This would also explain John's first recorded act. At the age of eleven years he ran away from home! How many a lad before and since has torn himself away from a loving mother's too fond embrace to quell the ardour of a restless spirit in the quest of adventure! John also was eager and dissatisfied; but the larger sphere for which he sighed was to be sought along the unaccustomed ways which lead to the sublime heights and the rarified atmosphere of mystic contemplation.

The pious truant made his way to Brussels, there to call upon an uncle of his, one John Hinckaert, a major Canon of St. Gudule's. The son and heir of a wealthy magistrate of the city, and possessed, moreover, of a rich benefice, for many years John Hinckaert had been somewhat worldly in his ways; but one day Divine grace found him out as he was listening to a sermon, and drew him sweetly and strongly to a life of extreme simplicity and mortification. His example was soon followed by a fellow Canon, by name Francis van Coudenberg, a Master of Arts, possessed of considerable means, and a man of great repute with the people. These two agreed, for their mutual edification and support, to live together in common. Their material requirements were reduced to the barest necessaries; and the surplus of their revenue was distributed among the poor. In this devout household the lad John met with a kindly welcome; and there he found at once a home after his own heart in an atmosphere saturated with " other-worldliness " and prayer. His good uncle also took charge of his education. For four years Ruysbroeck followed the ordinary course of Humanities in the public schools of Brussels, and then, with a view to the priesthood, he devoted himself to the more congenial study of the sacred sciences.

Meanwhile the bereaved mother had discovered the place of John's retreat and had quitted her village of Ruysbroeck to reside with him at Brussels. As, however, she was not permitted to dwell in the Presbytery, she made her abode in a *Béguinage* hard by.

Thus she had at least the consolation of seeing her son from time to time. She must have been much comforted also for the deprivation of his company by the constant evidence of his growing sanctity. And, further, we are assured that she set herself to make profit of her sacrifice by emulating in her own person the holy life of her son John, and his saintly masters, Hinckaert and van Coudenberg.

II

As a Secular Priest in Brussels

In due course Canon Hinckaert procured for his nephew one of the lesser prebends of St. Gudule's, and John was ordained priest in the year 1317, at the age of twenty-four. His good mother did not survive to witness this happy event in the flesh, nevertheless even beyond the grave she had good cause to rejoice therein. After her departure from this world she had often appeared to her son, lamenting her pains, beseeching his prayers, and sighing for the day when he would be able to offer for her the holy Sacrifice. And John was unceasing in his supplications. But immediately after the celebration of his first Mass, as he related to his Religious

Brethren later, God granted him a vision full of consolation: when the sacred oblation was accomplished, his mother came to visit and thank him for her deliverance from Purgatory. The touching incident is well worth recording, if only to show that it was through no lack of natural affection that the child John had so unceremoniously forsaken home and mother. Moreover, of these two holy souls it was singularly true that *having loved each other in life, in death they were not parted,* for they were privileged often to converse together, and finally it was from his mother that Ruysbroeck learned the date of his own approaching departure.

For twenty-six years in all Blessed John lived as a secular priest in Brussels. Content with his modest chaplaincy in the Church of St. Gudule, and with his holy companions Hinckaert and van Coudenberg continuing happily in apostolic simplicity and poverty the Common Life on which he had entered a mere child, Ruysbroeck passed his days in peaceful retirement and almost uninterrupted prayer and contemplation.

A characteristic episode of this period reveals to us the man as in a flash, his mean garb, his emaciated figure, his absorbed demeanour, his utter abandonment in God. He was passing through a square of Brussels one day, silent and recollected, as was his wont, when two laymen remarked him.

"My God," exclaimed one, "would I were as holy as that priest!"

"Nay, for my part," returned the other, "I would not be in his shoes for all the wealth of the world. I should never know a day's pleasure on earth."

"Then you know nothing of the delights

As a Secular Priest in Brussels

which God bestows, or of the delicious savour of the Holy Ghost," thought Ruysbroeck to himself, for he happened to overhear the words, and he proceeded tranquilly on his way.

III

FALSE MYSTICS

But with all his love of peace and retirement, when it was a question of guarding the integrity of the Faith and of warding off peril from immortal souls, Ruysbroeck hesitated not to stand in the breach; even though others of much higher position in the Church and of much higher repute for theological learning than the obscure chaplain of St. Gudule's should raise not a finger nor so much as utter a warning word.

The student of history is well aware of the many and startling contrasts and contradictions presented by the Middle Ages. It was an epoch of magnificent virtues and of gross vices, of splendid heroism and of unspeakable cruelty, of superb generosity and of disgusting meanness, and, which is more to our point at present, of intense devotion and of the most revolting vagaries in doctrine and morals. While also on the one hand there was much genuine zeal, much earnest endeavour to reform crying abuses in Church and State; on the other hand hypocrites and fanatics abounded, who aimed at the destruction of the principle of authority on the plea of amending those in power, or who, the while they inveighed against the futility of a merely exterior religion and insisted on the supreme need of purity of heart, themselves fell into the excess of neglecting all external form, and at times all outward decency and observance of morality.

In varying degrees these latter errors are to be encountered under one shape or another in every age ; but at the period of which we treat they were especially intense and extreme. The *Beghards* and the *Béguines* (when and where these broke loose from ecclesiastical control), the *Flagellants*, the *Brethren of the Free Spirit* were chief of a group of extravagant sects which afflicted the Church in Italy, France, Germany, and the Netherlands ; while England at the same time was disturbed by the fanaticism of the Lollards. In general their peculiar tenets were a strange admixture of pantheism, false mysticism, apparent austerity, and very real immorality. The following is one of their characteristic propositions, condemned by Clement V. in the Council of Vienna, A.D. 1311-1312 : " That those who are in the aforesaid grade of perfection and in the spirit of liberty (contemplatives) are not subject to human authority and are not obliged to obey any precepts of the Church, because (as they

False Mystics

say) *where the spirit of the Lord is, there is liberty.*"

It so happened that contemporary with our Saint in Brussels was a prominent leader of the heretics of the *Free Spirit*, a woman whose name is given as Bloemardinne, a good type, to judge by the description of Ruysbroeck's biographer, of the whole genus of such teachers in those days and in our own.* So great was this creature's reputation for sanctity that it was commonly reported that two Seraphim accompanied her to the altar when she approached to receive Holy Communion. She always delivered her teachings, whether by word or in writing, seated on a throne of silver. At her demise this chair was presented to the reigning Duchess of Brabant. After Bloemardinne's death

* *Cf.* the Polish sect of *Mariavites*, or *Mystic Priests*, under the misguidance of the woman Mary Frances, whose extravagances were condemned by Rome, September 1904, and again April 1906.

also cripples came to touch her body in the persuasion that they would be miraculously healed thereby. Her teaching was of the kind indicated above, concerned chiefly with the so-called liberty of the spirit; the passion of lust she had the impudence to call seraphic love. She issued numerous pamphlets remarkable for their subtlety; and by one means and another she managed to win and retain a very considerable number of disciples.

Moved by zeal and compassion on witnessing the ruin and loss of souls thus effected, John Ruysbroeck set himself to confute this heretic's various publications point by point as they appeared. In consequence, he incurred not a little hostility and persecution. Possibly it was this opposition which finally decided Ruysbroeck and his holy companions to quit Brussels for the more peaceful retirement of the neighbouring forest of Soignes.

But meanwhile he never for a moment desisted from his efforts in defence of the Faith, and in the propagation of the doctrines of sane mysticism. Of the treatises published professedly against Bloemardinne there is nothing extant. But in all his works Ruysbroeck keeps an eye on the errors of the day. He returns to them again and again, analysing their sources, describing their characteristics, indicating the mischief they work, and offering a reasoned and solid confutation. At the same time, with wondrous sureness and perspicacity, from the rich stores of his own intimate experience, he points out the safe and sure paths which lead the soul to loving union with God.

Some thirty years after Ruysbroeck's death, in 1410, the Archbishop of Cambrai called his disciples, the Canons Regular of Groenendael, to come and aid him in preaching against the successors of the notorious Bloemardinne—a fact eloquent both of the obstinacy of this particular heresy and of Blessed John's reputation as its most vigorous opponent.

IV

The Hermitage of Groenendael

It appears that it was on the suggestion of Francis van Coudenberg that the three holy priests resolved to abandon Brussels to seek elsewhere for themselves a refuge of greater security and retirement. It was through the influence also of van Coudenberg with John III., Duke of Brabant, that they obtained the cession of an ideal property for their purpose, the hermitage, namely, of Groenendael, with its lands and lake.

The spot had already been sanctified by the prayers and penances of holy recluses for nigh forty years. The first to retire thither had been one John Busch, of the ducal house of Brabant, who, weary of the strife, frivolities, and perils of court life, obtained from his kinsman, John II., leave to retire into the forest of Soignes, to build himself a hut and enclose a space of land there to be cultivated with his own hands for his support. The deed of gift was dated the Friday after the Assumption of Mary, 1304, and it stipulated that on the death or departure of the grantee, another hermit should take his place, and so on for ever. In effect, the noble John Busch was succeeded by one Arnold of Diest, who, on entering, made a vow never to sally forth save on festivals for the purpose of hearing Mass and receiving Holy Communion in the Parish Church of St. Clement at Hoolaert. God rewarded this generous sacrifice by a singular favour: Arnold was passionately devoted to the memory of the Holy Apostles and Martyrs of Rome, and he was transported in spirit so frequently thither that the shrines and sanctuaries of the Eternal City became as familiar to him as to a native. When in a green old age he came to die, Arnold surprised the bystanders with the request that he should be laid to rest in the hermitage grounds. They objected that the enclosure was not consecrated : he responded that one day it would be the site of a monastery, the home of saintly Religious, and the Mother-house of a holy congregation. However, he was buried in the Parish Church of Hoolaert before the altar of St. Nicholas. His successor, Lambert, the last of the Groenendael hermits, was so poor in spirit as not to be attached even to his cell. He cheerfully yielded place to John Hinckaert, van Coudenberg, and Ruysbroeck, and retired to a cell which they had procured for him at Hoetendael, the modern Uccle. Groenendael was handed over to the three companions by the Duke of Brabant on Easter Wednesday, 1343, on the condition that they should forthwith erect a house to accommodate a community of at least five, two of whom should be priests *viventes religiose*.

The taking of possession is recorded in the Groenendael Chronicle thus: "In 1344 the aforesaid, with the bishop's consent, began to build a chapel in Groenendael. And the Vicars of Lord Guy, then Bishop of Cambrai, inspected the building on March 13, 1344, and decreed that it should be consecrated, together with a cemetery adjacent, two altars, and other necessary appurtenances. On the same day of the same year the said Vicars conferred on Dom Francis the cure of the brethren, the household, and the servants, appointing him their Father and Parish Priest. Then the same year, on March 17, the Venerable Lord Brother Matthias, Bishop of the Church of Trebizond (Coadjutor of Cambrai), by faculty and licence of the said

Vicars of the Lord Bishop Guy, consecrated the aforesaid first church in the honour of St. James, and erected it into a Parochial Church for the same Dom Francis, his brethren and household."

For five years Dom Francis van Coudenberg and his companions continued to live thus in community, bound by no other rule than their own profound spirit of prayer and intense desire of perfection. Nor were they long left to enjoy alone the solitude of their retreat. Many sought admission into their company; still larger numbers flocked from Brussels and elsewhere to seek spiritual aid and consolation. If he had consulted his own inclination and bent, Ruysbroeck would have denied himself to all; but van Coudenberg represented that they should not in charity refuse assistance to souls in need. And Blessed John yielded the more easily, remarks one of his biographers, because for his part he was assured of being able to repose in God amid the most distracting calls and absorbing occupations.

One of their earliest associates, John van Leeuwen, attained a high reputation for sanctity. A poor and ignorant layman of Afflighem, he had offered his services as their domestic *gratis*. Before long he was known far and wide as the " Good Cook of Groenendael." The multitude of visitors upon whom he was called to attend left him but little leisure, yet he found time not only to be absorbed in prayer and contemplation, but even to compose treatises of an exalted spirituality. Like his master Ruysbroeck, whom he venerated profoundly, he was deeply recollected amid the most exacting duties, and frequently he was favoured with heavenly visions. It was while in a state of ecstasy that the sublime gifts and heroic holiness of Blessed John were revealed to him; ever after no terms seemed to him too exalted in which to describe the worth of the servant of God. The general esteem in which van Leeuwen himself was held is sufficiently attested by the inscription on his tomb: "Reliquiae Fratris Joannis de Leeuwis vulgo Boni Coci viri a Deo illuminati et scriptis mysticis clari obiit anno MCCCLXXVII. V. Februarii." *The Remains of Brother John van Leeuwen, commonly called the Good Cook, a man enlightened by God and renowned for his mystic writings. He died February 5, 1377.*

Much more distracting to the recluses than the frequent visits of pilgrim penitents or the arrival of fresh neophytes was the constant coming and going of huntsmen from the household of the Duke of Brabant. The forest of Soignes, in which Groenendael is situate, was a favourite resort for the chase, and the position of the hermitage itself, within a few miles of the capital, made it a very convenient place of rest and refreshment for the hunters and their hounds. But the noise and bustle attendant on such company were scarcely conducive to the spirit of prayer, and the demands thus made on the hospitality of the young Community were a heavy drain on its resources. Nevertheless the solitaries were naturally fearful of giving offence to the followers of their Patron the Duke. Moreover, since they were not established as a regular Religious Community, they could not claim the privileges of the cloister.

V

THE CANONS REGULAR OF GROENENDAEL

THE inconveniences just noted, together with the continual increase in their numbers, gave point and force to a strong remonstrance addressed to Francis van Coudenberg and his Brethren by Pierre de Saulx, Prior of the Canons Regular of St. Victor, Paris, concerning the *irregularity* of their unaccustomed manner of life. Herein the good Prior was in effect only voicing the opinion of many zealous and prudent leaders among both clergy and laity. The times were so rife in sects and societies of false mystics, and so much mischief was wrought under the guise of piety, that any form of community life outside the cloister and the three regular vows was regarded with strong suspicion and dislike. A few years later Gerard Groote, a disciple of Ruysbroeck, and Florence Radewyn, the first spiritual Director of the Venerable Thomas à Kempis, founded a lay association of *Devout Brothers and Sisters of the Common Life,* and this society also was subjected to a fierce opposition arising from the same sentiment of distrust for all religious movement outside the beaten track. Happily, the Brothers were able to weather the storm by producing irrefragable proofs of their orthodoxy, and of their entire submission to the ecclesiastical authorities. But also, by the advice and according to the desires of Gerard Groote himself, they placed themselves under the protection and guidance of a Religious Order springing from their own body, namely the Canons Regular of Windesheim, of which congregation the Venerable à Kempis was one of the earliest members as well as the brightest ornament.

Prior Pierre de Saulx urged on van Coudenberg and his associates to regularise their status, silence suspicion, and escape the many inconveniences to which at present they were exposed by embracing the Rule and adopting the habit of some already established Religious Order. With edifying humility the Community of Groenendael accepted the reproof and its accompanying counsel; and applied at once to Peter Andrew, Bishop of Cambrai, for the necessary authorisation to adopt the Institute of the Canons Regular under the Rule of St. Augustin of Hippo. This permission the Ordinary granted most readily. With his own hands he clothed Francis van Coudenberg, John Ruysbroeck and their companions in the canonical habit, March 10, 1349, and the following day he appointed Dom Francis Provost,* and John Ruysbroeck he made Prior of the new Canonry. To van Coudenberg the other members of the Community, with one exception, professed canonical obedience, according to St. Augustin's Rule. The Bishop bestowed upon them many privileges and exemptions; while the Duke took them under his special protection and endowed them with sufficient revenues for the upkeep of a large establishment.

The one exception noted above was Ruysbroeck's uncle and van Coudenberg's old friend and master, John Hinckaert. At this date John Ruysbroeck was fifty-six years of age, and Francis van Coudenberg was several years his senior. They must certainly have been men of great zeal and courage to

* Provost is the equivalent in a College of Clergy of the Abbot in a Monastery; though many Congregations of Canons Regular have borrowed the title and style of Abbot from the monastic institute.

undertake the full rigour and discipline of the Canonical Life, as they understood it, at so advanced an age. Hinckaert, again, was much older than either. And for fear lest out of consideration for his failing powers the others should be induced to temper in any degree the austerity of their observance, the good old man resolved to forgo for himself the happiness of joining them in the profession of the vows. We can picture what a source of regret this separation must have been to all three. However, Hinckaert remained as near his friends as possible until the end. A little cell was built just outside the cloister, and there after a few years he peacefully passed away, their predecessor to eternal glory as he had been their forerunner in the way of perfection.

The Canon Regular, Prior Pierre de Saulx, had reason to be well content with the issue of his intervention in the affairs of Groenendael. Seventeen years later we find him addressing to the Community another characteristic rebuke. This time he complained of the formula of their profession, which ran as follows: " I, N. , offer and deliver myself with these gifts to the service of this Church of St. James, Apostle. And I promise God in the presence of clergy and people that I will abide here henceforth to the end of my days without proprietorship, according to the rule of the Canons and Blessed Augustin, to the best of my knowledge and power. I also promise stability to this place as long as in any way I can obtain what is needful for my soul and body, nor shall I for any motion of fickleness or under any pretext of a more strict Order change this habit or quit this cloister. I also promise obedience to all the prelates of the aforesaid Church whom the better part of the Community shall canonically elect, in order that I may receive a hundredfold and life everlasting."

As a matter of fact, this form of profession was quite adequate. Implicitly it contained the vow of chastity, since chastity is an integral part of the Canonical Rule. However, the Prior of St. Victor resided in Paris, the metropolis of scholasticism, and he strenuously argued and maintained that, whereas chastity is one of the three essential vows of Religion, and the formula made no mention thereof, the said formula was incomplete, erroneous, contrary to the decretals and canonical sanctions. And again he urges the Provost and the Brethren to conform themselves in this, as in all else, to some fully authorised branch of the institute of the Canons Regular.

Once more the good men humbly acquiesced ; and it seems that they modelled their religious family upon the famous Congregation of St. Victor, of which their zealous counsellor was then the chief Superior.

VI

Prior of Groenendael

Meanwhile the Community of Groenendael grew and flourished. The holy Prior continued to make progress in the practice of heroic virtue, his gifts of contemplation became ever more sublime, and still his reputation for sanctity increased. His contemporary biographers, after the fashion of their day, catalogue the Christian virtues, and one by one show how they excelled in him. Let it suffice here to remark that those virtues which he the most earnestly commends and the most highly exalts in his writings, he the most constantly exercised in his own person. Chief of these was humility, which he terms everywhere the foundation of perfection; then obedience to men and resignation to the will of God, a most tender devotion towards Jesus Christ in the Blessed Sacrament of the Altar, and, in fine, an ardent love of God and the neighbour. A few instances may be given in illustration.

On one occasion Blessed John was seriously ill; consumed by fever and tortured by an intense thirst, he begged the Brother Infirmarian for a drink of water. The Provost, who happened to be present, forbade the draught, fearing it might do him harm. He was literally dying of thirst, and his lips were cracking, they were so parched, yet Ruysbroeck humbly acquiesced. But later, reflecting how great would be the grief and remorse of his friend and superior if he actually died of his agony, he quietly remarked: "Father Provost, if I have not a drink of water now I shall certainly not recover from this malady." Thereupon, in great alarm, Dom Francis immediately bade him drink. And from that moment the holy man began to regain his strength.

Another and a continual proof of his humility was the willingness with which he took part in the heavy manual labour of the Community. His dignity, his advanced age, his inexperience in such work, the many other calls upon his time and strength—all this and the like the brethren urged as motives wherefore he should be exempt; but he refused to listen. Truth to tell, the material advantage from his toil was but little: his frame was enfeebled by years and austerities, and in his ignorance he was liable, for instance, to root up seedlings in the garden instead of weeds! But the spiritual gain to the Brethren was incalculable; there was not only the example of his humility, but of his unfailing recollection too. In the midst of his labour he never lost his sense of the nearness of God's presence. Indeed he was wont to say that it was easier for him to raise his soul to God than to lift his hand to his forehead.

His humility also and his zeal for the regular observance prevented him ever seeking dispensation from the customary exercises of the community life, or exemption from any of the monastic austerities, vigils, or fasts.

His love for the neighbour was shown by the readiness and affability with which he received and welcomed innumerable claimants on his sympathy, help, and counsel. No soul ever left his presence dissatisfied ; every one went back from a visit to Groenendael greatly edified and inwardly refreshed. On one occasion the Brethren were distressed for the moment by an apparent exception. Two Parisian clerics had visited the holy old man and had demanded some word or motto for their guidance and encouragement.

Ruysbroeck merely observed: "You are as holy as you wish to be." Suspecting him of sarcasm, the strangers retired deeply mortified, and they complained to the Canons that they were much disappointed in the Prior, who evidently was not so saintly a man as rumour had led them to believe. Learning the cause of their chagrin, some of the Brethren led the clerics back to Blessed John and begged him to explain his meaning. "But is it not simple?" he cried. "Is it not quite true? You are as holy as you wish. Your good-will is the measure of your sanctity. Look into yourselves and see what good-will you have, and you will behold also the standard of your holiness." And then the visitors retired appeased and edified.

Naturally his own Brethren were the first

and chief to benefit by the holy Prior's charity and zeal. He denied himself to none, he made himself all to all. Sometimes he gave a spiritual conference after Compline, and then perhaps he would be so carried away as he enlarged upon the goodness of God and the bliss of heaven, for instance, that neither he nor his listeners would note the passage of time. The midnight Office bell would surprise them still hanging upon his words. But such was the fervour infused by his burning eloquence that not one felt the loss of the three or four hours' accustomed sleep.

Ruysbroeck always spoke without any immediate preparation; but it was characteristic of the man that when requested by the Canons or by strangers for a Conference, he would sometimes confess in all simplicity that inspiration was lacking, that he had nothing to say. It was the same with his written treatises: at the close of his life he was able to declare that he had never committed anything to writing save under the immediate motion of the Holy Spirit.

As so often happens with the Saints, Blessed John's love for the neighbour overflowed in tenderness for his brothers and sisters of the lower creation also. Knowing this trait, the Canons would remark to him on the approach of winter: "See, Father Prior, it is snowing already. What will the poor little birds do now?" And with expressions of heartfelt compassion this sublime mystic, who was habitually lost in dizziest heights of contemplation, would give instructions that the feathered choristers outside the cloister should not be abandoned to perish of hunger.

Very frequently in his works Blessed Ruysbroeck takes occasion to treat of the Holy

Sacrament of the Altar, and ever he speaks of this sacred mystery in terms of the most vivid faith and intense devotion, discussing it as a supreme proof of God's love for men, on a par with the gifts of Creation, the Incarnation, and Redemption. His biographers tell us of his personal love for the Blessed Eucharist, and especially of his ecstatic devotion in offering the great Sacrifice. To the close of his long life, even when his failing sight could no longer distinguish the figure of the Crucified stamped upon the Host, nothing but grave sickness could hold him back from daily celebration. Sometimes he swooned from the excess of the sweetness with which his soul was inundated during the canon of the Mass.

On one such occasion not only did he faint, but he seemed on the point of expiring, so that the terrified server reported the matter to the Provost. Attributing the faintness to advancing age and weakness, the Superior was about to forbid the holy old man to celebrate any more, when Blessed John humbly besought him to forbear, assuring him that the swoon was due not to the failing of years but to the overpowering of divine grace, *non propter senium sed divinae gratiae collatum xenium.* " Even to-day," he added, " Jesus Christ appeared to me, and filling my soul with a deliciousness all divine, He said to my heart, *Thou art Mine and I am thine.*"

Such heavenly favours seem to have been by no means rare with our Saint. He was frequently ravished with a vision of Our Divine Lord in His sacred Humanity. Christ appeared to him, accompanied by His Blessed Mother and a numerous retinue of Saints, and conversed familiarly with him. On one such occasion, penetrating his whole being with a sense of wondrous sweetness, He greeted him with ineffable condescension thus: "Thou art My dear son, in whom I am well pleased." Then Jesus Christ embraced him and presented him to Our Lady and the attendant Saints with the words: "Behold My chosen servant!"

VII

Ruysbroeck's Tree

WHENEVER Blessed John felt the Spirit of God full upon him, even the solitude of the cloister was not sufficiently retired for the intimacy of the divine union. He would wander away into the depths of the forest surrounding the monastery, there to abandon himself to the action of the Holy Ghost undisturbed. On these occasions also he was wont to take with him a stylus and a wax tablet, in order to jot down such thoughts and lights as he was moved to preserve in writing. Of these notes a fair copy was made on his return to the Priory. Towards the end of his days, when his sight was failing and otherwise the effort of making these notes was too much for him, one of the Canons always accompanied him into the forest to write down at his dictation whatever he was moved to communicate. Sometimes days or whole weeks would pass, and for want of inspiration not a line nor a word would be added to the treatise in hand. But when again the Spirit breathed, he continued from the very sentence or phrase where he had paused, just as if there had been no interval between.

One day the Saint had retired as usual into the forest, and the Brethren, knowing his occupation, respected his privacy. But when hours passed and there was no sign of his return, they became alarmed and set out to scour the woods in search of him. One of the Canons was especially intimate with the Prior and loved him most tenderly. Perhaps his anxiety urged him ahead of the rest. In a glade of the forest his eye lighted upon a wondrous scene. He perceived a tree as it were in flames. On nearer approach he discovered that it was in fact encircled with fire. And under the tree, in the midst of the mysterious conflagration, John Ruysbroeck was seated, manifestly rapt in ecstasy.

The memory of this miracle was never lost in the Community. For generations the tree was known and venerated as *Ruysbroeck's Tree*. At the close of the fifteenth century the Prior, James van Dynter, planted a lime-tree in the same place, which received the respect shown hitherto to the original, which presumably had died down. When in 1577 the Canons were obliged to abandon Groenendael on account of the vexations of the religious wars, it is said that this tree withered away until only its bark was left ; but when the Community returned in 1607, it revived and flourished again.

This episode also has fixed the traditional representation of Blessed John Ruysbroeck.

He is usually pictured seated under a tree, a stylus in his hand and a wax tablet resting on his knee, while Saint and tree alike are encircled in brilliant rays of celestial light.

VIII

A Director of Souls

It is no wonder that as the fame of these and similar marvels spread abroad, multitudes of the faithful, young and old, clergy and laity, flocked to see and hear the holy Prior of Groenendael. They came to him from Flanders, Brabant, Holland, Germany, and France. Ruysbroeck received all with unvarying simple courtesy, and his unpremeditated words were ever found to meet exactly the needs of each. Many placed themselves unreservedly in his hands, and frequently sought his direction by correspondence, or came long distances to consult him in person.

One of these penitents was the Baroness

van Marke, of Rhode-St.-Agatha, which lies midway between Groenendael and Louvain. This lady conceived such a veneration for the holy Prior that when she went to visit him, she walked the journey, pilgrimwise, barefoot. Finally, his exhortations to flee and despise the passing vanities of the world prevailed so much with her that she entered a Convent of Poor Clares in Cologne, and her son Ingelbert joined the Community of Groenendael.

We are told of another disciple, who once fell into a grievous sickness and at the same time into a still more grievous affliction of spirit. She sent for Blessed John, begging him to visit her. She told him of her distress; behold, she was abandoned by God, on the one hand no health or strength was left her to perform her accustomed works of mercy, and on the other hand physical suffering took away all taste for prayer! What was she to do? "You can do nothing more pleasing to God, my dear child," responded the Saint, "than simply and utterly to submit to His holy will. Strive to forsake your own desires and to give Him thanks for all things." Such unction accompanied these simple and characteristic words that the good lady felt deeply consoled, and she repined no more.

Among the more famous to frequent Groenendael, there to sit and learn at the feet of Ruysbroeck, is mentioned the well-known German mystic Tauler. But authorities are divided at present as to whether or no these visits to Groenendael can be fitted in with other ascertained facts of Tauler's life. However, it is certain that Tauler was well acquainted with the writings of our Saint; to a great extent he followed his method, and at times, in the free-and-easy style of those days, he did not hesitate to transfer bodily from Ruysbroeck's volumes into his own.

IX

Ruysbroeck and Gerard Groote

A GREATER than Tauler, and one whose influence was eventually far more widespread, undoubtedly owed much to the recluse of Groenendael and freely acknowledged Blessed John his master. This was the famous Gerard Groote, the founder, as already noted, of the *Devout Brothers and Sisters of the Common Life,* and through them of the Windesheim Congregation of Canons Regular. The occasion and circumstances of Groote's first visit to Groenendael are narrated by the Venerable Thomas à Kempis in his *Vita Gerardi Magni.* The passage is so graphic and characteristic that it is well worth transcribing.*

* Translation by J. P. Arthur. *The Founders of the New Devotion.* Kegan Paul. 1905.

"The pious and humble Master Gerard, hearing of the great and widespread fame of John Ruysbroeck, a monk and Prior of the Monastery of Grünthal, near Brussels, went to the parts about Brabant, although the journey was long, in order to see in bodily presence this holy and most devout Father; for he longed to see face to face, and with his own eyes, one whom he had known hitherto only by common report and by his books; and to hear with his own ears that voice utter its words from a living human mouth— a voice as gracious as if it were the very mouthpiece of the Holy Ghost. He took with him therefore that revered man, Master John Cele, the director of the School of Zwolle, a devout and faithful lover of Jesus Christ; for their mind and heart were one in the Lord, and the fellowship of each was pleasant to the other, and this resolve was kindled within them that their journey, which was undertaken for the sake of spiritual edification, should redound in the case of each to the Glory of God.

"There went also with them a faithful and devout layman, named Gerard the shoemaker, as their guide upon the narrow way, and their inseparable companion in this happy undertaking.

"When they came to the place called Grünthal, they saw no lofty or elaborate buildings therein, but rather all the signs of simplicity of life and poverty, such as marked the first footsteps of our Heavenly King, when He, the Lord of Heaven, came upon this earth as a Virgin's Son, and in exceeding poverty. As they entered the gate of the monastery, that holy Father, the devout Prior, met them, being a man of great age, of kindly serenity, and one to be revered for his honourable character. He it was whom they had come to see, and saluting them with the greatest benignity as they advanced, and being taught by a revelation from God, he called upon Gerard by his very name and knew him, though he had never seen him before. After this salutation he took them with him into the inner parts of the cloister, as his most honoured guests, and with a cheerful countenance and a heart yet more joyful showed them all due courtesy and kindness, as if he were entertaining Jesus Christ Himself.

"Gerard abode there for a few days conferring with this man of God about the Holy Scriptures; and from him he heard many heavenly secrets which, as he confessed, were past his understanding, so that in amazement he said with the Queen of Sheba, 'O excellent Father, thy wisdom and thy knowledge exceedeth the fame which I heard in mine own land; for by thy virtues thou hast surpassed thy fame.' After this he returned with his companions to his own city, greatly edified ; and being as it were a purified creature, he pondered over what he had heard in his mind and often dwelt thereon in his heart ; also he committed some of Ruysbroeck's sayings to writing, that they might not be forgotten.

" This sojourn on his visit to the Prior was not a time of idleness, nor was the discourse of so holy a father barren ; but the instruction of his living voice gave nurture to a fuller love and an increase of fresh zeal, as he testifies in a letter which he sent to these same brethren in the Grünthal, saying : ' I earnestly desire to be commended to your director and Prior, the footstool of whose feet I would fain be both in this life and in the life to come; for my heart is welded to him beyond all other men by love and reverence. I do still burn and sigh for your presence, to be renewed and inspired by your spirit and to be a partaker thereof.' "

Other details of this interesting visit are supplied by the biographers of Ruysbroeck. Speaking in the fullness of the intimacy that had sprung up between them, Gerard Groote ventured to express surprise that, in dealing with the sublime matters which usually formed the subject of his discourse, the holy Prior should employ words and phrases which laid him open to the charge of those very errors, especially pantheism, against which his writings were commonly directed. It was then that Ruysbroeck declared that he had never set down aught in his books save by the inspiration of the Holy Ghost and in the presence of the Ever Blessed Trinity. This solemn assurance the holy man repeated to his brother Canons on his deathbed.

On another point also, like the trained and exact theologian he was, Gerard Groote wished to correct his friend. He insisted that the boundless confidence which Ruysbroeck expressed in the mercy of God seemed to savour somewhat of presumption, and he proceeded to quote the most terrifying passages from Scripture anent the penalties of the wicked. Blessed John quietly replied: "Master Gerard, I assure you that you have quite failed to inspire me with fear. I am ready to bear with unruffled soul whatever the Lord shall destine for me in life or in death. I can conceive of nothing better, nothing safer, nothing more sweet. All my desires are restricted to this, that our Lord may ever find me prepared to accomplish His holy will."

This first visit was the beginning of most cordial relations between Ruysbroeck and Gerard Groote. The latter returned several times to Groenendael and resided there for months together. He also corresponded frequently with the holy Prior and the Canons and translated some of our Saint's works into Latin. He read over his MSS. before publication, and begged him at times to change or modify expressions which might give a handle to the hostile or scandal to the weak. The writings of Ruysbroeck were likewise among those which were the most frequently transcribed and multiplied by the copyists of the *Devout Brothers of the Common Life.* A few years later one of the most diligent and skilled of these scribes was the future author of the *Imitation of Christ.*

X

RUYSBROECK AND WINDESHEIM

IN fact, widespread as was the influence of Blessed John Ruysbroeck on his contemporaries and incalculable as was the fruit of his writings in the many cloisters, through which they were rapidly diffused, the means by which Divine Providence chose chiefly to preserve and propagate his power was precisely this friendship with Gerard Groote. Gerard continually strove to imbue his own disciples with the spirit which he had imbibed from the Prior of Groenendael. For himself and for his followers he took as a rule of life the motto of Ruysbroeck, *to make it a chief study to meditate upon the life of Jesus Christ.* "Let the fountain-head of thy study and thy mirror of life be first the Gospel of Christ, for there is the life of Christ." The Scriptures should be read rather than the Fathers, and the New Testament more than the Old, *for there is the life of Christ.* And herein again what is profitable for a devout and spiritual life is to be sought rather than the subtleties of theology and the schools.

When a friend of Gerard's, Reinalt Minnenvosch, projected the founding of a monastery, Groote advised him to establish a Priory of Canons Regular on the model of Groenendael. The Canonry of St. Saviour's at Emstein was the result. At Groote's request, a professed priest came from Groenendael to initiate the new Religious into the Canonical Life; and later it was at Emstein that the first members of Gerard's own Congregation of Windesheim made their noviciate preparatory to Profession.

This was after Gerard Groote's death, but it was in accord with his express desire. Wishful to establish a Religious Institute in connection with his *Devout Brothers and Sisters of the Common Life*, who, whether lay or cleric, were dwelling together without the binding force of the vows, Gerard fixed upon the Order of Canons Regular for this purpose, principally, so Thomas à Kempis assures us, because of his profound veneration for the Prior and Brethren of Groenendael. "He was moved to institute this Order of Regulars chiefly by his singular reverence and love for the venerable Dom John Ruysbroeck, the first Prior of Groenendael, and of the other most exemplary Brethren living there religiously in the Regular Order."

For further information concerning the *Devout Brothers* and the Windesheim Canons the reader is referred to the various works which have been published of late years on the Venerable à Kempis.* Both Brothers and Canons were living examples of the mystic teachings of Ruysbroeck put to the test of daily practice. Flight from the pleasures and vanities of the world, unbounded humility, constant meditation on the life and especially the Passion of Jesus Christ, the most complete and absolute abandonment to the Divine Will, an intense devotion full of the personal love of God— these were the salient points of Blessed John's example and doctrine, perpetuated and propagated by the works, words, and writings of the Windesheim Canons Regular and their

* Especially : *Outlines of the Life of Thomas à Kempis.* By Sir Francis Cruise. C.T.S. of Ireland. *Thomas à Kempis.* By the same. London : Kegan Paul. *Life of the Venerable Thomas à Kempis.* By Dom Scully. London : Washbourne. *Thomas à Kempis and the Brothers of the Common Life.* By Kettlewell. London : Kegan Paul. *Thomas à Kempis, His Age and His Book.* By De Montmorency, London : Methuen.

secular associates, the *Brothers of the Common Life*. It is scarcely needful to remark also that these are the chief features of the teaching of the *Imitation of Christ*, that golden little treatise, which, embodying the whole spirit of the School of Windesheim and Groenendael, has carried and still carries light, healing, and consolation to thousands upon thousands who have never so much as heard of either Windesheim or John Ruysbroeck.*

* Father Sharpe, in his recent admirable volume, *Mysticism: Its True Nature and Value*, writes thus of the mystic teaching, properly so called, of à Kempis's world-famous masterpiece: "*The Imitation of Christ* . . . probably owes much of its vast popularity to its constant recurrence to the elementary duties of religion and morality, and its insistence on the necessity of their performance as the prerequisite of the more exalted spiritual states. The 'purgative,' 'illuminative,' and 'unitive' ways are seen, so to speak, together, and are dealt with as aspects or constituents of the Christian life as a whole, to the completeness of which all three are necessary and, in different ways, of equal importance. The purely mystical passages are comparatively few and short; and the abun-

It may be mentioned here that in 1409 the Priory of Groenendael was instituted the Mother-house of a congregation of that name. But a few years later this congregation, with its dependent Priories, was affiliated to the more numerous Windesheim Canons. Thus the twin institutes were merged into one, and the Windesheim Congregation be-

dance of practical directions the book contains has sometimes caused its mystical character to be entirely overlooked. This disproportion, however, is quite sufficiently to be accounted for by the character of the work, which is that of a directory of spiritual life in general, and not a scientific treatise on any particular department of it. In such a book attempts at describing the indescribable phenomena of mysticism would obviously have been out of place, whereas the practical details of the lower and preliminary states admit of and require minute explanation. But the tone of the whole book is mystical, and the most commonplace duties and the most humiliating strivings with temptation are in a manner illuminated and glorified by the brilliancy of the result to which they tend. Thus, in point of fact, the higher and lower elements, the mystical and the non-mystical, the purgative, the illuminative and the unitive, are blended in actual human experience" (pp. 188, 189).

came the direct heir of the virtues and teaching of Blessed John Ruysbroeck. But finally Windesheim was aggregated to the Lateran Congregation of Canons Regular; and thus it is that to-day the Canons Regular of the Lateran are privileged, with the clergy of Mechlin, to keep with proper Office and Mass the Feast of Blessed John Ruysbroeck.

Connected thus intimately with Gerard Groote and Tauler, it is not surprising that Ruysbroeck shares with these, as with à Kempis, Suso, and others, the doubtful honour of being proclaimed in certain quarters as a precursor of the sixteenth-century "Reformation." In support of this position it is easy enough to gather together expressions of the most poignant sorrow and of the most bitter invective for the lax morality of clergy and laity, mendicant friars, and highly placed prelates. But the same argument would convict several Popes of being heralds of Luther! Not to labour the point at unnecessary length in a non-controversial work of this kind, let it suffice to mention the touchstone which never fails to distinguish the genuine reformer from the mere sectarian: while boldly attacking the vices of those in office, Blessed John Ruysbroeck never assails the office itself. He always speaks in the most submissive and reverent terms of the authority of the Church and of the dignity of the priesthood. His writings without exception treat in the orthodox sense on the subject of grace, the sacraments, etc. We have already remarked his ardent devotion towards the Blessed Eucharist. To this may be added a most tender love for the Virgin Mother of God. Note, finally, his frequent and fervent exhortations to the perfect observance of the three vows of religion, and one can imagine how comfortable he would feel in the company, say, of Luther and his renegade nun!

XI

The Writings of Ruysbroeck

Blessed John's writings cannot be called voluminous, and yet for a purely contemplative author they are comparatively considerable. The list of his works authenticated up to the present—for earnest students are at work, and other MSS. may yet be discovered—comprises the following, giving an English equivalent for the Old Flemish or Latin titles: (1) The Kingdom of the Lovers of God; (2) The Splendour of the Spiritual Espousals; (3) The Brilliant; (4) Of Four Subtle Temptations; (5) Of the Christian Faith; (6) Of the Spiritual Tabernacle; (7) Of the Seven Cloisters; (8) The Mirror of Eternal Life, or, a Treatise on the

Blessed Sacrament; (9) The Seven Degrees of Spiritual Love; (10) Of the Supreme Truth; (11) The Twelve Béguines. And these others are less certainly proved to be his: (12) Of the Twelve Virtues; (13) Seven Letters; (14) A Summary of the Spiritual Life; (15) Two Canticles; (16) A Short Prayer.

Pending a complete and faithful English rendering of all these works, the following descriptive analysis of the principal of them may not prove unacceptable.

The Kingdom of the Lovers of God

This treatise is a detailed interpretation and a mystic application of the text adapted from Wisdom x. 10: *Justum deduxit Dominus per vias rectas et ostendit illi regnum Dei* in the Breviary Office of a Confessor. Upon these words Ruysbroeck bases a division of his work into five books. The first book treats of God, *Dominus*, His power and sovereignty. In the second Blessed John explains how Christ conducted, *deduxit*, man into the liberty of the children of God, chiefly by redemption and by the institution of the seven Sacraments. In the third he treats of the just man, *justum*, and works out eight items which render a man just, both in the active and in the contemplative life. The fourth book expounds the right ways, *vias rectas*, which lead to the Kingdom of God: *the exterior way*, namely, the material universe of three heavens and four elements, the contemplation of which should excite man to the praise of the Creator; *the way of natural light*, the acquisition of the seven virtues; finally, *the supernatural and divine way*, the infusion of the supernatural virtues and the gifts of the Holy Ghost. In the last book we have a disquisition on the kingdom of God, *ostendit illi regnum Dei*, of which we are told there are five aspects or divisions: the sensible kingdom, exterior to God, in which the author finds scope for a description of the last judgment and the qualities of risen bodies, the kingdom of nature, the kingdom of the Scriptures, the kingdom of grace and of glory, and finally the Divine Kingdom itself, which is God. This treatise is full of reflections and considerations of the most elevated order, and there is much therein that is by no means easy to grasp or understand.

The Splendour of the Spiritual Espousals

For his text Ruysbroeck takes Matt. xxv. 6, *Ecce, sponsus venit, exite obviam ei*. He makes a division into three books, treating respectively of the active, the interior, and the contemplative life. Each book is further subdivided into four parts, corresponding to the four divisions of the text in each stage of perfection as follows. Ruysbroeck expounds and illustrates (1) the rôle of the vision, *ecce*; man must turn his eyes to God; (2) the divers comings of the Bridegroom, *sponsus venit*, the manner, namely, in which God approaches the soul; (3) the going forth of the soul on the path of the virtues, *exite*; (4) and finally, the embrace of the soul and the heavenly spouse. In no one work does Blessed Ruysbroeck give a complete account of his mystic teaching; but if his system were to be examined and explained by any one book, it would certainly be this of the *Spiritual Espousals*. It has always been considered as his chief work, and in this light also Ruysbroeck himself seems to have regarded it. He sent a copy of it himself to his friends in Germany, and expressed the desire that it might be multiplied and made known even to the foot of the mountains. In the four last chapters of the second book the author confutes some current errors of the day, apparently the teachings of Bloemardinne and almost certainly of Eckart.

The Brilliant

Gerard Naghel tells us the story of the origin of this treatise. One day Ruysbroeck had been conversing with a certain hermit on matters spiritual, when on parting the latter begged the holy Prior to commit the matter of his discourse to writing for the edification of himself and others. To satisfy his desire, says Naghel, Ruysbroeck composed this work, which contains instruction sufficient to lead a man to perfection. The treatise seems a supplement, and in some sense a corrective of the *Spiritual Espousals*. After a brief description of the means by which the just man acquires the interior life and rises thence to the contemplative, the holy man shows how the precious stone, or white counter, *calculus candidus,* of Rev. ii. 17, is no other than Christ Himself, Who gives Himself without reserve to contemplative souls. God calls all men to intimate union with Himself. But not all men respond to His appeal. Sinners utterly despise the invitation; while the just respond, though these again in varying degrees. Some keep the commandments chiefly from fear of the penalties attached to transgression; they are as *mercenaries.* Others sincerely endeavour to conquer nature and unruly desires, they have true faith in God, and God is the only motive of their actions; these are the *faithful servants.* However, these still suffer many impediments from the exterior life which they lead, and a more intimate union is attained by the *intimate friends,* who observe the counsels as well as the precepts. Finally, the highest degree of union and contemplation is attained by the *hidden sons*, who are utterly divested of all self-love and self-seeking, and whose life is hidden with Christ in God.

Of Four Subtle Temptations

In this tract Ruysbroeck inveighs against the chief errors and abuses of his own times. The first, says Ruysbroeck, is love of ease and comfort, indolence, the source of sensuality, and luxury, an abuse very prevalent in monasteries and among the clergy. The second is hypocrisy, which, under the cloak of a seeming austerity, claiming even visions and ecstasies, conceals a corrupt interior and depraved morals. The third is the desire to understand everything, to attain to the contemplation of the divine nature by the sheer force of the intellect, without the assistance of God's grace. The fourth and most formidable is the so-called *liberty of spirit*, the error and heresy of those who, casting aside all interior effort, pretend to acquire contemplation by ludicrous mortifications, by extravagant bodily posturing, and by a senseless quietism. The third error is that of Eckart, and the fourth was proper to the Brothers and Sisters of the Free Spirit. Ruysbroeck concludes his tract with a discussion of the ways and means of avoiding these snares, viz. by holiness of life, the practice of all the virtues, obedience to superiors and the authority of the Church, and imitation of Jesus Christ.

Of the Christian Faith

A dogmatic commentary on the Athanasian Creed. Starting with the principle that the true Christian Faith is indispensable for the union of the soul with God, Ruysbroeck proceeds to explain the chief tenets of our belief, and to show their bearing on the interior life. His explanations are brief, his speculations sublime. The more forcibly to exhort to the practice of virtue, he dwells at considerable length on the last judgment, on the rewards of the just, and on the penalties decreed to each particular class of sinner. His picture here of the happiness of heaven and the sufferings of hell is most apt and striking.

Of the Spiritual Tabernacle

The most lengthy this of all Ruysbroeck's works. It consists of a mystic interpretation, a long-drawn-out allegory, in which the Tabernacle of the Old Testament is considered as a type of the course of love.

The outer and the inner courts, the altar of sacrifice, the hangings, the pillars and their sockets, the rings, the names of the workmen, the seven-branch candlestick, the brazen laver, the priestly ornaments, the ephod and the twelve stones, the holy oils and the incense, the table of the loaves of proposition, the different sacrifices with the distinction between the clean and the unclean animals, the holy of holies, the ark and its appurtenances,—all are applied with a wealth of detail, which, however, never lacks dignity, and with a wondrous skill to Ruysbroeck's usual three divisions of the exterior moral life, the interior, and the purely contemplative. The Tabernacle was a subject which naturally lent itself to allegory and to mystic interpretation, and Hugh of St. Victor had already preceded our author, as doubtless also he inspired him with his *De Arca mystica.*

Though sometimes the thread is lost in the multiplicity of details, this treatise is most attractive and contains some of the best pages of Blessed Ruysbroeck.

Of the Seven Cloisters

This was composed for a penitent of our Saint, Margaret von Meerbeke, a Poor Clare of Brussels, and it gives a rule of life for Religious. The holy Prior traces out an order of the day, insisting especially on the need of cultivating the interior life; he mentions the virtues which his penitent should exercise, and inveighs against the abuses which have crept into convents, pointing out the danger of communication with the outer world. In all things Margaret should imitate the example of her foundress, St. Clare, who gained her glorious place in Heaven by shutting herself up within the seven cloisters. After dwelling on these, viz., by expounding seven means of retreating from the world and living close to God, the author turns again to practical details and condemns the softness and luxury of certain Religious in their dress. Each day, he says, should close with a peep into three books: the book of our own conscience, which shows the imperfections which must be purified; the book of the Life and Passion of our Lord, which we should imitate; and finally the book of eternal life, to which we ought to tend with all our strength.

The Mirror of Eternal Life

This also was addressed to a nun, probably the same Poor Clare. It explains again the three degrees of the mystic life, but with special reference now to the cloister and the

Blessed Eucharist. Some are in the purgative way: if they persevere in virtue and progress in perfection, they shall partake of the table, Ps. xxiii. 5, which is no other than the banquet of the Holy Eucharist. Ruysbroeck dwells on the virtues necessary for the worthy reception of the Sacrament, and narrates the manner of its institution by our Divine Lord at the Last Supper, showing what were the matter and form used by Christ. He discourses on the evidence of God's love to be found in this mystery of the altar; and then refutes objections as to the manner of the Divine Presence, expressly teaching Transubstantiation. Those who approach the altar rails are divided by him into seven classes, and here the author shows a wondrous and intimate knowledge of the working of the human heart. The treatise closes with a description of the contemplative life.

The Seven Degrees of Spiritual Love

In a simile familiar to spiritual writers of all ages, Ruysbroeck compares life to a ladder, or stairway of seven steps, leading up to perfection and union with God. These stages are respectively: (1) Conformity with the holy will of God; (2) Voluntary poverty; (3) Purity of soul and chastity of body; (4) Humility, with her four daughters, obedience, gentleness, patience, and the forsaking of self-will; (5) The desire of the divine glory, involving three spiritual exercises, namely, acts of love and adoration, acts of supplication, and acts of thanksgiving; (6) The contemplative and perfect life, by which man finally attains the last stage of, (7) sublime ignorance. (Compare Walter Hilton's "darksome lightness" in his *Scale of Perfection*.)

Of the Supreme Truth

This treatise was issued by way of explanation of some difficult passages in his first work, concerning especially the gift of counsel, and indeed as a kind of defence and apology of his whole mystic teaching. He protests that he has never admitted that the creature can be raised to a state of identity with God, and once more he explains his conception of the union of the soul with her Divine Spouse. There is a union common to all the just, brought about by the grace of God, with the forsaking of vice, the practice of virtue, and submission to the authority of the Church. Then there is a more intimate union, like unto that of fire and iron, which, when united, seem but one matter, though in fact they remain two distinct substances. Those who attain this love God and live in His presence, but as yet arrive not at a complete knowledge of His essence. After this again there is even a yet closer union, whereby the Eternal Father and man become one, not indeed with oneness of substantial unity, but in a oneness of love and bliss. It is evident that language here fails the holy author to express the sublimity of his concept and his experience; in his endeavour to show the intimacy of this last method of union he is driven to use expressions which, taken as they stand, have that pantheistic ring which it is his first object here to disclaim.

The Twelve Béguines

After the *Tabernacle*, this is the most lengthy of our Saint's works, and it is of great importance as throwing considerable light on Ruysbroeck's ideas and system. We are introduced to twelve Béguines discoursing together on the love of Jesus Christ, whence an easy transit to the real subject-matter of the tract, the contemplative life. To attain the state of contemplation, four conditions are required: a ray of divine light, producing illumination, whence, on the part of the soul, a looking at God, or speculation, passing into contemplation, and this stage again merging into a state of sublime, ecstatic love. There are four distinct acts or states of love, corresponding respectively to each of these stages. Ruysbroeck also shows here the action of the Holy Ghost in forming the soul to a more intimate knowledge of God.

The second part of the book then opens with a fresh order of ideas. Ruysbroeck divides mankind into good Christians and wicked men. Holiness consists of the union of the active and the contemplative life. There are, however, some who practise neither one nor the other and yet give themselves out as the most holy of all. Among these Ruysbroeck proceeds to distinguish four kinds of errors or heresies: (1) Errors against the Holy Ghost and His Grace; (2) Errors against God the Father and His power; (3) Errors against God the Son and His Sacred Humanity; and finally errors against God and all that makes up Christendom, namely, the Scriptures, the Church, and the Sacraments. On the other hand, the good Christian is one who loves God with all his heart and mind and soul and strength.

Blessed John then goes on to discourse of the Divine Nature in Unity and Trinity. He also discusses man in his material and in his spiritual nature. The spiritual part of man alone, he says, can elevate him to the mystic life (of which once more the three ways are expounded), and alone also can show him the reasons wherefore God created the universe. The three ways of the mystic life are symbolised by the three heavens. The stars and the planets exercise an influence on terrestrial creatures, that is to say, upon our bodies, for God alone can touch the soul, leading it to good and restraining it from evil. Thence also Ruysbroeck describes the various temperaments of men by reference to the planets and their conjunction with the signs of the zodiac.

A chapter on our Divine Lord, held up as the Model Religious, serves as a transition to the third part, which is a treatise, largely symbolical, on the Passion of Christ, divided and subdivided according to the sequence of the Canonical Hours.

This is perhaps the most discursive of Ruysbroeck's works, and in that sense the most difficult to follow, because of the number and length of the digressions. For instance, when he comes to speak of the planet Venus, he mentions the sign of the Balance, and this suggests a whole treatise of thirty-nine chapters on the *Balance of Divine Love*. The love of God for us, and all the blessings, spiritual and temporal, which flow from it, are cast into one pan of the balance, and we must weigh down the other pan with our virtues; and there follows a long disquisition on the virtues we should practise, prominent among which, as usual, he ranks humility. Here, further, he finds occasion to work out his distinction between the spirit and the reasonable soul; and the whole digression closes with a sad and striking comparison between the fervour of primitive Christianity and the laxity of his own days.

Bossuet very severely criticised this work, holding it up as an example of forced allegories, and so forth, and speaking of Ruysbroeck as involved in the vain speculations of astrologers. This opinion, though not surprising, is not just, for the author is careful to insist that the planets have not influence on the will of man as such. But it is natural that Bossuet should regard such works with suspicion and dislike, for he had considerable trouble with false mystics, the quietists of his own day ; and even Ruysbroeck's own friends and contemporaries found much in the volume that was strange, even to startling, and Gerard Groote advised him not to publish it in its entirety.

Of the Twelve Virtues

The reader will not be surprised to learn that Blessed John contrives here to speak of considerably more virtues than just twelve. The principal and first is said to be humility, and this again twofold—one humility inspired by the contemplation of the power of God, the other by the consideration of His goodness. The daughter of humility is obedience, and obedience naturally involves denial of self-will, poverty of spirit, and patience in adversities. He then proceeds to treat very beautifully and at length of interior detachment, remarking that to secure this it is not necessary to flee external occupations, but that the attainment of perfection consists in a perfect abandonment to the will of God and the forsaking of our own will. When we have arrived thus far, we shall no longer sin. For past sins there must be continued sorrow, but external penances are not equally for all. And those who cannot endure great bodily austerities must apply themselves to imitate the austere life of Christ by interior self-denial.

The Letters of Ruysbroeck

These are spiritual letters, of course, conferences in epistolary form.

The first is addressed to Margaret van

Meerbeke, the Poor Clare of Brussels mentioned above. Ruysbroeck writes: "When I was at your convent last summer, you appeared sad; methought God or some special friend had forsaken you; therefore am I writing you as follows." And he proceeds to console his spiritual daughter, and to warn her against the dangers which may be found even in the cloister. He declaims against the abuses which sometimes creep into monasteries, and almost always through *self-will*, whereas every Religious should strive to have all things *in common*, to be submissive to superiors and affable to all. The holy author closes with a description of the terrible punishments to be meted out to those Religious who fail to keep their rule and lead a holy life.

The second, addressed to Matilda, the widow of John of Culemberg, is of more importance. After treating of the Apostles'

Creed, the seven gifts of the Holy Ghost, the Decalogue, the vows of religion and the precepts of the Church, the Incarnation and death of Christ, Ruysbroeck expounds the Catholic doctrine on the seven Sacraments, and especially the Blessed Eucharist. He describes the fruits which flow from a worthy Communion, and treats again of the three ways of the contemplative life, and describes the elements of superessential contemplation.

The third was sent to three Recluses of Cologne. Blessed John exhorts them to persevere in their holy manner of life. He treats of the spiritual life, comparing Christ to the precious pearl, the hidden treasure. And finally he earnestly exhorts them to constant meditation on the Passion of Our Lord.

The fourth was addressed to Catherine of Louvain, a devout young lady living in the world ; and the other three were likewise sent to persons in the world. All are full of wise spiritual maxims, and all insist on the need of humility and the abnegation of self-will.

XII

The Teaching of Ruysbroeck *

In no one work, as already remarked, does Blessed John Ruysbroeck give a complete outline of his doctrines; the elements rather are to be found dispersed among the various treatises.

In common with most of the German mystics, Ruysbroeck starts from God and comes down to man, and thence rises again to God, showing how the two are so closely united as to become one. In His essence God is simple unity, the one supremely pure

---

* The whole subject of mystic theology is excellently well treated by Rev. A. B. Sharpe, M.A., in a volume entitled *Mysticism: Its True Nature and Value*, already quoted, just published by Sands & Co. There is frequent reference to our Saint and his writings.

and supernatural being, devoid of all mode, in Himself still and immovable, and yet at the same time the first cause and active principle of all things. This principle is the divine *nature*, which does not in reality differ from the essence, and which is fruitful in the Trinity. The Father is the essential principle, and yet He is consubstantial with the other two Persons. The Son, the uncreated Image of the Father, is the Eternal Wisdom. The Holy Ghost, proceeding from the other two, and returning unto them, is the eternal Love, which unites Father and Son. As regards Persons, God is eternally active: as regards essence, He abides in unbroken repose. Creatures have been existing as ideas in God from all eternity.

In man, whose body is merely a perishable instrument, there is a spiritual, immortal principle, like unto God, though less than He. In this principle Ruysbroeck distinguishes, with a distinction of the reason, soul and spirit; the former is the principle of the merely human life, uniting together the lower powers; the other is the principle of man's supernatural life in God, gathering together his higher faculties. The soul has four inferior powers: the *irascible*, and the *concupiscible*, which two become bestial when not under the ruling of a virtuous will; *reason*, by which man is distinguished from the brute, and *freedom of choice*, an exercise of the higher faculty of the will. The spirit has the three superior faculties, memory, understanding, and will. In every man likewise there is a triple unity, or oneness: the unity of the lower faculties in the soul, the unity of the higher in the spirit, and the unity of the whole being in God, on Whom all things essentially depend for their being.

Blessed John delivers the accepted teaching of the Church on the Fall, the Incarnation and

Redemption, on the need and on the means of divine grace, the institution of the Sacraments, the establishment of the Church, the gifts of the Holy Ghost, etc.

But coming now to his more purely mystical doctrine, we find that Ruysbroeck distinguishes three degrees, or states—the active life, the interior life, and the contemplative life. The active life consists of the effort to conquer sin and to draw nigh to God by exterior works. Here in Christ is the Divine Exemplar, for in His life He practised the three fundamental virtues of humility, charity, and patience. Humility is the foundation of the whole building, and it is exercised chiefly in obedience, which engenders the abdication of our own will, and patience, or submission in all things to the holy will of God. When a man has arrived so far, he can exercise charity, shown at this stage chiefly by compassion for Christ suffering on the Cross for all men, and bringing with her the four cardinal virtues of prudence, temperance, fortitude, and justice, whereby also the Christian is enabled to fight and conquer his three deadly enemies, the devil, the world, and the flesh. Perseverance in this active life is crowned by union with God, a union wherein God alone is regarded as the exemplar and the final end, wherein He alone is sought and loved. Thus does a man become a *Faithful Servant*.

As yet, however, there is only an imperfect knowledge of God, and to become more closely united with God, as an *Intimate Friend*, one must strive to attain the second stage of the mystic way, namely the *interior life*. For this three preliminary conditions are requisite. On the part of God, there must be a yet stronger movement of divine grace, and on the part of man, an absolute recollection, with freedom from sensible images, attachments, and cares, and then the gathering together of all the powers in the unity of the Spirit. Christ, then, the Eternal Sun, enkindles in the soul thus duly prepared a divine fire, which engenders a warm, sensible love, a devotion full of ardent desires, with thankfulness for the divine mercies and affliction at one's own unworthiness. Then, as the action of the sun draws up the moisture in the form of vapour, to fall back again in refreshing and fertilising showers of rain, so if the soul persevere Christ sends down a fresh shower of consolations, which fill the whole being with a chaste pleasure and an indescribable sweetness, superior to all the delights of the earth, rising even to a species of spiritual intoxication, which may manifest itself in outward acts. As yet there are no severe trials for the soul, but she must beware of pride and presumption, and of leaning too much on these sensible delights instead of on the Divine Giver. Meanwhile the Sun of

Justice is reaching its apogee in the heavens, and Christ draws up all the powers of the soul, so that the heart is enlarged and fit to burst with love, and at the same time it begins to suffer from the wound of love, because of the urgency of the power drawing upward and its own impotency to follow; whence also a spiritual languishing, a very madness and impatience, or fever of love, capable even of wasting the bodily strength. Love is liable to be so intense at this stage, that visions and ecstacies are granted; but at the same time care must be taken against the delusions of the evil one.

But thence the Sun enters on the sign of the Virgin and its downward path, that is, Christ hides Himself and deprives the soul of the warmth of sensible love and the like. It is the autumn, the time of gathering the really ripe and lasting fruits; but to the soul a time of seeming abandonment, aridity, darkness, etc. She must then beg the prayers of others, be glad to leave herself in God's hands, willing to suffer and to sacrifice all sweetness. Likewise, she must be careful not to compromise God's favour by seeking earthly pleasures and delights, the consolations of human friendship, and so forth.

Then there is a second coming of the Divine Spouse, bringing with Him the gifts of the Holy Ghost, whereby He adorns the three supreme faculties of the spirit. Pure simplicity empties the memory of all external images and renders it stable. Spiritual brightness gives the intelligence a sure discernment of the virtues. And a spiritual fervour arouses the will to a boundless love for God and men.

There is yet a third coming, which affects the supreme union of the spirit with God. It is a species of intimate contact with God in the very depths of the soul. The intellect cannot comprehend the manner of this union, it can only witness its effects upon the reason and the will. The power of loving increases with the intimacy of this union, and the intimacy increases the power of love; and hence also a kind of loving strife ensues, each wishing to possess the other and each wishing to give himself to the other utterly.

This is the apogee of the interior life, the meeting, the union of the soul with God. It may be brought about in three different ways: (1) Man, struck by a light coming forth from God, forsakes all images; he is plunged into the union of fruitive love; he meets God without any medium, a spirit like unto Him; it is the state of absolute repose in God, utter emptiness and leisure. (2) At other times man adores God and consumes himself in continual love, which ceaselessly feeds on the presence of God; it is the mediate stage, the state of affective love, needful for the attainment of the preceding. (3) Finally, it is possible to unite enjoyment with activity: man enjoys a most profound peace and produces all the acts of love; he receives God and His gifts in the superior faculties, images and sensations in the lower powers; it is the most perfect state, the state of combined activity and repose.

Even so, it is not the most sublime state. Above the interior life there is the superessential contemplative life; above the *faithful friends* there are the *Intimate Sons* of God. This third stage of perfection can never be acquired by any act of the intelligence or will; and so sublime is it that he only who has experienced it can attempt its description, and then in terms the most halting and imperfect. This contemplation consists in an absolute purity and simplicity of the understanding; it is a knowledge and possession of

God, without modes, without limits, without medium, without any consciousness of the difference of His qualities. Nevertheless, it is not God, it is the light by which He is seen. It is the death and destruction of self to behold only the Being eternal and absolute. Its essence is union with God, the still contemplation of God, abandonment to God, so that He alone acts, and not the soul. This repose of the spirit engenders a supernatural contemplation of the Trinity without any medium, a feeling of bliss unspeakable, a sublime ignorance; the last consciousness of the difference between God and the creature —being and nothingness—disappears.

This is the honeymoon of Christ with the soul, to which the preceding stages are only a preparation. The spirit is led from brightness to brightness; and since no medium comes between it and the divine splendour, since the brightness by which it sees is the light itself which it sees, in a certain sense itself becomes this brightness; it attains a consciousness of its own superessential being, of the unity of its essence in God.

XIII

Some Appreciations

Arrived thus at the summit of mystic speculation, Ruysbroeck finds himself on the confines of pantheism. However, he constantly insists, as we have already remarked, on the essential difference between the created spirit and the Spirit Eternal. Man, he says, must become deiform as far as that is possible for the creature; in the union with God it is not the difference of personality which is destroyed, it is only the difference of will and of thought, the desire to be anything apart in oneself which must disappear. He declares: " There where I assert that we are one in God, I must be understood in this sense that we are one in love, not in essence or in nature." His own strenuous opposition to the pantheists of his day proves his orthodoxy in this matter; yet it must be confessed again that from the very nature of his sublime discourse, his expressions are at times exceedingly bold and seemingly unorthodox. The truth is that the resources of human language prove inadequate to describe even the foretaste on earth of that "which eye hath not seen, nor ear heard, nor hath it entered into the heart of man to conceive."

In B. John's own lifetime Gerard Groote was alarmed, and wrote once to the Canons of Groenendael of a Doctor in Theology, and of one Henry of Hesse, who had declared that the *Spiritual Espousals* contained errors. Twenty years after Ruysbroeck's death, John Gerson, the famous Chancellor of Paris, in a letter to one Bartholomew, a Carthusian, who had given him a copy of this treatise, praises the first two books, but declares that the third teaches a kind of pantheism. This charge brought forth a lengthy and spirited defence from a Canon Regular of Groenendael, named John Scoenhoven; and then in a second letter Gerson maintained his objections, but acquitted the holy author of all intentional error. A similar stand was taken later by Bossuet, who excuses Ruysbroeck but condemns his manner of expression. It must be remembered that these two were engaged in confuting false mystics, and naturally they would discredit the writings of even a holy man, however orthodox, which would appear to favour the erroneous tenets of their opponents. Once more, we remark that not only was Ruysbroeck manifestly free from all culpable error, but throughout in his own mind he never lost sight of the essential distinctions, though at times his language must necessarily sound exaggerated to unaccustomed ears.

On the other hand, to outweigh the unfavourable opinion of these two French critics, we have a host of writers of Ruysbroeck's own and subsequent days who not only defend the orthodoxy of his writings, but who also speak of them in terms of the deepest admiration, and regard their author almost as inspired.

We have already seen the esteem in which the holy Prior of Groenendael and his writings were held by Tauler, Gerard Groote, and the Venerable Thomas à Kempis, and the vigour with which his memory was vindicated by John of Scoenhoven. But his advocates were by no means confined to the limits of his own Order, period, or country.

Henry van Herp, a Franciscan, compiled a *Mirror of Perfection*, taken almost exclusively from the *Spiritual Espousals*; and by his means the teachings of Blessed Ruysbroeck were propagated among the followers of St. Francis, particularly of the Third Order.

Denys the Carthusian is unstinted in his praises. He calls him the *Divine Doctor*. "I name him the Divine Doctor," he writes, "because his only master was the Holy Ghost. Of this the abundance of wisdom wherewith he was gifted is a sure guarantee. . . Ignorant man as I am, I confess that nowhere have I found such sublimity and such knowledge, save in the works of Denys the Areopagyte. But in his writings the difficulty arises especially from the style, whereas it is not so with the Prior of Groenendael. . . . As they say of Hugh of St. Victor that he is another St. Augustin, so I will say of Ruysbroeck that he is another Denys the Areopagyte."

Thomas of Jesus, a Carmelite, in his *De Divina Oratione*, frequently quotes from Ruysbroeck and adopts his method.

The Carthusian Surius translated all the

works of Ruysbroeck into Latin, and this translation has been the chief source of familiarity with the Belgian mystic for readers and writers not acquainted with his native tongue. The following extracts from the *Introduction* to Surius's translation seem worth quoting for the sake of some who may imagine that the works of Blessed John Ruysbroeck can be of profit only to those who are far advanced in the contemplative life :

" I do not believe there is a man who can approach these magnificent and simple pages without great and singular profit. Let none excuse himself from reading this book on the plea of the inaccessible sublimity of Ruysbroeck. The great man has accommodated himself to all, and the most abandoned soul on earth may find again on reading him the path of salvation. Arrows dart from the pages of Ruysbroeck, aimed by no hand of man, but by the hand of God ; and deeply they embed themselves in the soul of the reader who is a sinner. Innocent reader, reader of unstained robe, Ruysbroeck is at once most lowly and most sublime. In his description of the *Spiritual Espousals* he surpasses admiration, he surpasses praise; all the commencement, all the progress, all the height, all the transcendent perfection of the spiritual life is there."

It was from Surius that the Benedictine Blosius, or Louis de Blois, learned to know and appreciate Ruysbroeck. His works are impregnated with the teachings of the Mystic of Groenendael, and his well-known *Consolatio Pusillanimum* (*Comfort for the Fainthearted*) is replete with extracts taken from Ruysbroeck.

Lessius, the Jesuit Theological Professor of Louvain University, used to say that he read Blessed John Ruysbroeck daily; and he would add that if his holy works had emanated from the Society they would not have remained in obscurity so long.

In more recent times Ernest Hello brought our Saint to France by a translation of extracts, prefaced by an anonymous contemporary life, which was first published in 1869. In his own *Introduction*, Hello writes: "Among those who, soaring beyond the realms of human light, have sought refuge in the shadow of the great altar, the grandest, according to Denys the Carthusian, are St. Denys the Areopagyte and John Ruysbroeck the Admirable. St. Denys lays down the general laws of mystic theology, John Ruysbroeck applies them. St. Denys presents the lamp, John Ruysbroeck kindles the flame. Both are blind with excess of light, both immovable with excess of motion. Speech with them is a visit paid to men from motives of charity. Silence is their native land. The beauty of their language is the condescendence of their goodness ; the sacred darkness in which they spread their eagle wings is their ocean, their booty, their glory."

Reviewing the work of Hello, Louis Veuillot, the French Catholic publicist, remarked :

" Ruysbroeck was illiterate. He was a humble Flemish priest of the fifteenth century. None the less, in the order of genius the uncultured Ruysbroeck, as a theologian, and consequently as a philosopher and a poet, is as far above Bossuet as Dante, for instance, is above Boileau. Face to face with the mysteries that shroud God and man, Bossuet seeks, argues, and, so to speak, gropes ; Ruysbroeck knows, describes, or rather sings, and contemplates. This illiterate mystic of an obscure age finds himself at home in the sublime as in his own sphere ; he speaks of what is familiar to him ; the wise doctor of the world remains without. Bossuet does not enter, he does not open, he does not see.

Bossuet spins words, Ruysbroeck pours out streams of light. It seems as if Bossuet were that mighty wind which was heard in the Upper Chamber; the brief words of Ruysbroeck are the tongues of fire, living and enlightening flame."

Truly has Time brought its revenge in such a comparison by a compatriot of Bossuet with Ruysbroeck.

Finally, Maeterlinck brought out his translation of the *Spiritual Espousals* in 1891 with a characteristic appreciation of the Flemish mystic. And Maeterlinck's name has given a strong impetus to the popularity, so to speak, of Blessed Ruysbroeck in modern France. But neither of these translations can be regarded as authoritative or exact.

The real, scholarly work towards extending and encouraging the cult of Blessed John Ruysbroeck, whether among the learned or the devout, is being performed, as is seemly, in the Catholic University of his native Belgium, namely, at Louvain, where a Chair has been instituted for the study of Old Flemish, chiefly for the sake of a correct understanding and rendering of the writings of the Holy Mystic of Groenendael.

And here we may note that while it is customary with some to speak of Ruysbroeck as illiterate, this term must be taken in a strictly limited sense. Possibly, he could not have composed in fluent and elegant Latin: he was not a classical scholar; but certainly the Latin of the Bible and the Fathers was quite familiar to him. His writings, moreover, display an intimate knowledge of the Scriptures, the Fathers, theology, liturgy, apologetics. The natural science of the day was not unknown, as witness his applications from astronomy, and, it must be confessed, from astrology. With St. Denys the Areopagyte he shows himself very intimate, and his pages contain whole passages borrowed or adapted from St. Anselm, St. Ambrose, St. Gregory, and especially St. Augustin. Nearer his own days St. Bernard and Hugh of St. Victor seem to have influenced him very considerably.

Experts in Old Flemish assure us that his style is most chaste, his language vigorous and clear. He was in truth a poet. When carried away by the beauty or sublimity of his subject, he indulges in a wealth of imagery, comparison, metaphor, astounding at times in boldness and originality. Occasionally even he lapsed into verse ; but on the whole his verse is of less beauty and strength than his prose, as he himself seems to have been aware. On the other hand, his prose, after the manner of St. Bernard, St. Bonaventure, the two Victors, and later Thomas à Kempis, frequently gives evidence of deliberate rhythm and rhyme. In a word, far from being illiterate in the strict sense of the word, Blessed John was well acquainted with all the rules and arts of rhetoric ; he knew how to employ them ; and for all the sublimity of his discourse he did not disdain the use of these aids to interest and persuasion. Finally, it is to be noted that we are expressly informed by contemporaries of Ruysbroeck that he wrote by preference in the vulgar tongue, the more readily and effectively to meet and refute the erroneous doctrines published in the language of the people by the false mystics of his day.

XIV

Last Days

Of the life of our Saint there remains little to be told save the record of the last days and the after glory. He had attained the good old age of eighty-eight, when his mother appeared in a vision to warn him to make ready for the approaching end. It must seem to us there was little need for such warning to one whose whole life had been one long preparation for the coming of the Spouse! He was taken with dysentery, accompanied by fever, and for his greater comfort, and that his lifelong friend van Coudenberg might be at hand to console and assist him, they put him to bed in the Provost's chamber. But the humble Prior besought them to treat him as any of the lowliest brethren and to bear

Last Days 119

him to the common infirmary. This was accordingly done. There he lay for a fortnight, gradually wasting away with the burning fever, and still more, doubtless, with his burning desires to be dissolved and to be with Christ, for he was constantly heard murmuring such ejaculations as that of the Psalmist, *Sicut desiderat cervus ad fontes aquarum.* He received all the last rites, and the end came in the greatest peace, while his weeping brethren prayed around him, on the Octave day of St. Catherine, V.M., December 2, 1381, in the eighty-eighth year of his age, the sixty-fourth of his priesthood.

That same night the Dean of Diest, watching by the holy remains, seemed to behold our Saint, clad in the priestly vestments and all radiant with glory, ascend the altar steps as if to celebrate the sacred mysteries. The Dean had always held Ruysbroeck in the deepest veneration and, having some skill in medicine, he had come over to Groenendael on hearing of the Prior's illness to see whether he could administer any relief. His charity was rewarded by the edifying sight of his happy death, and by this consoling vision after.

And, as the Venerable à Kempis informs us, "God also revealed to Gerard [Groote] the death of this most beloved Father, which revelation he made manifest in the hearing of many of the citizens by the tolling of the bells; and more privately he made known to certain of his friends that the soul of the Prior, after but one hour of Purgatory, had passed to the glory of Heaven." We may note here that à Kempis himself was a child of three years when Ruysbroeck was called to his reward. Gerard Groote followed his friend and spiritual father to the grave three years later.

The Groenendael Canons offered the holy

Last Days

Sacrifice and all the wonted suffrages for their departed Prior's repose, but they prayed with the conviction that they needed his impetration rather than he theirs. They were all eager to possess themselves of any little thing which had been his. Some cut off locks of his hair, and one managed to secure a tooth! Appropriately enough, this relic later cured a Mechlin lady of a severe attack of toothache. However, in all simplicity the Brethren laid Blessed John to rest in the little chapel which his own hands had helped to raise.

Five years later his saintly associate, the Provost Francis van Coudenberg, rejoined him beyond the grave. The Bishop of Cambrai, John T'Serclaes, came to assist at the obsequies. During his visit he heard so much of the heroic virtues of the late Prior that he ordered an exhumation of Ruysbroeck's body with a view to a more honourable burial by the side of the Provost in the new church, which had now replaced the little chapel. They were all filled with awe and wonder to find the entire body, save only the tip of the nose, incorrupt, and the priestly vestments intact. Also a most sweet odour exhaled from the holy remains. To satisfy the devotion of the people, the Bishop commanded that the body should be exposed to their veneration for three days. On the third day, amid a vast concourse of the faithful, Ruysbroeck was laid to rest by the side and in the tomb of his lifelong friend van Coudenberg. Over the sepulchre was placed the following simple inscription:

Hic jacet translatus Devotus Pater
D. Joannes de Ruysbroeck
I. Prior hujus monasterii
Qui obiit anno Domini
MCCCLXXXI
II. Die Decembris

"Here lies transferred the Devout Father, Dom John of Ruysbroeck, First Prior of this cloister, who departed in the year of the Lord 1381, December 2."

XV

THE CULTUS OF BLESSED JOHN RUYSBROECK

NUMEROUS pilgrims now wended their way to visit Ruysbroeck's tomb. Ex-votos were suspended there in acknowledgment of favours received. His picture also was honoured in various churches. And each year on the Monday following Trinity Sunday the Chapter of St. Gudule's came over to Groenendael to assist the Canons at a Mass sung in his honour. In a word, on all sides the holy Prior was regarded and, as far as possible, treated as a Saint in glory.

Yielding to representations and entreaties from many quarters, James Roonen, Archbishop of Mechlin, ordered another translation of the remains, November 1622. This was duly performed with all the prescribed formalities. The skeleton was found entire. The bones were carefully taken and reverently washed and then placed in a new reliquary. The water used in this cleansing emitted a delicious odour, and it was afterwards instrumental in effecting many miraculous cures. The Infanta Isabella of Spain laid the foundation stone of a chapel to be erected at her expense near *Ruysbroeck's Tree* as a suitable shrine for the relics. She also provided a magnificent sarcophagus. As this chapel was outside the monastic enclosure, ladies were now able to pay their devotions at Ruysbroeck's tomb itself, whereas hitherto they had been able to reverence the relics only from a distance.

So far, however, no authoritative recognition of the heroic virtues of John Ruysbroeck had come from Rome. In 1624 the Archbishop commissioned the learned Albert le Mire to draw up the necessary preliminary documents to be submitted to the Sacred Congregation. These were approved, and three commissioners were appointed to initiate the apostolic process, so called. Their labours were completed by 1627. Then, on account of the wars and other troubles which afflicted the Low Countries at the time, the Cause was suspended.

When the French overran the Netherlands in 1667, to prevent profanation of the holy relics, they were carried to a place of greater safety in Brussels; they were restored again in 1670. In 1783 the Priory itself shared the fate of so many other Religious Houses, and was suppressed by the Emperor Joseph II.; whereupon the relics were again transferred to Brussels and laid to rest in a side-chapel of St. Gudule's.

Another attempt was then made by the Chapter of St. Gudule's to obtain from Rome an authorised Office and Mass in honour of John Ruysbroeck. The petition was favourably received; but once more there was a violent interruption, this time from the upheaval of the French Revolution.

St. Gudule's was sacked by the *sans-culottes* in 1793, and the reliquary of Ruysbroeck was desecrated. It is said, however, that the relics were not actually dispersed, and that they were afterwards sealed up again by a Notary named Neuwens; but unhappily at the present day all trace of them has disappeared.

Finally, in 1885, the late Cardinal Goosens, Archbishop of Mechlin, approached the Sacred Congregation once more, and a tribunal was appointed to examine into the Cause, February 8, 1900. This was brought to a happy issue in 1908 by a Decree of the Sacred Congregation, dated December 1st, and approved by His Holiness, Pius X., December 9, confirming the cultus " shown from time immemorial to the Venerable Servant of God, John Ruysbroeck, Canon Regular, called the Blessed." Later, August 24, 1909, the Congregation granted and approved an Office and Mass of Blessed John Ruysbroeck for the Mechlin clergy. The privilege of this Office and Mass has also been extended to the Canons Regular of the Lateran, who are the lineal representatives of the Canons of Groenendael and Windesheim, and therefore in a special sense the children of Blessed John.

For the moment there may seem to be but little in common between this Mediæval Mystic and the bustling modern world, so little as to suggest the thought that Blessed Ruysbroeck can have no message to deliver to our day. On the contrary, the Solitary of the Forest of Soignes stands for a profound truth, oblivion of which is rendering Society sick unto death to-day. John Ruysbroeck preaches to the world its utter need of God.

For the Catholic he enforces his lesson in a special manner. Unlike false mystics, who invariably pretend to dispense themselves and their adherents from the chief normal means of grace, namely the Sacraments, Ruysbroeck insists upon frequent recourse to the Sacraments, but more especially to the Blessed Eucharist, as the speediest and most efficacious means of bringing each soul into true union with God. Our present Holy Father, desirous and ambitious of "restoring all things in Christ," has pointed to the same divine remedy for the renewal of our souls. May there not be seen in this a providential reason wherefore the solemn beatification of this holy Religious has been delayed six centuries, to be reserved to our own days?

The proper prayers of our Saint's Mass

beautifully summarise the lessons of his life as follows:

Collect

O God, Who didst vouchsafe to adorn Blessed John, Thy Confessor, with sublime holiness of life and with heavenly gifts, grant us, through his merits, and after his example, to despise the fleeting things of the world, and to desire only the joys of heaven.

Secret

May the intercession of Blessed John, who in offering the Sacrifice merited to overflow with heavenly delights, make us worthy, we beseech Thee, Lord, of the bread of angels.

Post-Communion

We beseech Thee, O Lord, by the intercession of Blessed John, grant to us who are refreshed with the heavenly banquet, that, delivered from worldly desires, we may be ever fervent in Thy love.

FINIS

PRINTED BY
HAZELL, WATSON AND VINEY, LD.,
LONDON AND AYLESBURY.